LANDMARK TOP TENS

The World's Most Amazing
Dams

Ann Weil

Chicago, Illinois

www.heinemannraintree.com

Visit our website to find out more information about Heinemann-Raintree books.

To order:

☎ Phone 888-454-2279

🖳 Visit www.heinemannraintree.com to browse our catalog and order online.

© 2012 Raintree
an imprint of Capstone Global Library, LLC
Chicago, Illinois

Customer Service: 888-454-2279
Visit our website at www.heinemannraintree.com

Edited by Megan Cotugno and Laura Knowles
Designed by Victoria Allen
Picture research by Hannah Taylor and Ruth Blair
Original illustrations © Capstone Global Library Ltd (2011)
Production by Camilla Crask
Originated by Capstone Global Library Ltd
Printed in China by CTPS

15 14 13 12 11
10 9 8 7 6 5 4 3 2

Library of Congress Cataloging-in-Publication Data
Weil, Ann.
   The world's most amazing dams / Ann Weil.—1st ed.
      p. cm.—(Landmark top tens)
   Includes bibliographical references and index.
   ISBN 978-1-4109-4244-9 (hc)—ISBN 978-1-4109-4255-5
(pb) 1. Dams—Juvenile literature. I. Title.
   TC540.W45 2012
   627'.8—dc22   2010038410

Acknowledgments
The author and publishers are grateful to the following for permission to reproduce copyright material: Corbis pp. 4–5 (© Du Huaju/Xinhua Press), 11 (Frans Lanting), 12 (Zheng Jiayu/Xinhua Press), 23 (Reuters), 18 (© Marc Garanger), 19 (David Trilling), 26; Getty Images pp. 10 (Adriano Machado/Bloomberg), 15 (Lester Lefkowitz), 22 (John Scofield/National Geographic), 24 (Popperfoto); PA Photos p. 25 (AP Photo); Photolibrary pp. 7 (Meredith Castlegate), 6 (Cuboimages/Federico Maneghetti), 13 (JTB Photo), 27 (Peter Arnold Images/Mark Carwadine); Shutterstock pp. 8 (© Andy Z), 9 (© iofoto), 14 (© Benedictus), 16 (© JoLin), 20 (© S.E.V).

Cover photograph of the Hoover Dam, Lake Mead Reservoir, in Colorado, Arizona, and Nevada, USA reproduced with permission of Alamy Images (USA © imagebroker).

We would like to thank Daniel Block for his invaluable help in the preparation of this book.

Contents

Some words are printed in bold, **like this**. You can find out what they mean in the glossary.

Dams

A dam is a structure that blocks water in a river and prevents it from flowing downstream. This usually creates a pond or lake behind the dam. Beavers build dams so they have a pond to live in. People build dams for several reasons.

Many cities depend on these large lakes, called **reservoirs**, for their water supply. Dams can be part of a power plant, too. The flow of water is used to **generate** electricity. Some dams are huge, but most are small. You may live near a dam without even knowing it!

Flood control

When rivers overflow their banks, land and homes may end up underwater. Floods can be a big problem for some people who live near rivers.

Dams can control the flow of water so a river no longer floods. Extra water is held back in lakes or reservoirs. Then water is released slowly over time. People use the **artificial** lakes created by dams for fishing, swimming, and boating.

Dams can be used to control water flow in areas where floods are a problem. This photo shows flood water from the Yangtze River being released at the mighty Three Gorges Dam in China. The Three Gorges is one of the world's largest dams.

Aswan Dam

The Aswan Dam spans the Nile River in the middle of the Egyptian desert. The Nile River used to overflow its banks about once a year. These floods helped keep the soil good for growing crops. But some years there was too little rain. Then the river did not flood. This could be a disaster for the Egyptian people who needed the water for their crops, farm animals, and themselves.

Aswan Dam

Location: Aswan, Egypt

Size: 6 trillion cubic feet (170 billion cubic meters)

That's Amazing!
This dam created Lake Nasser, the world's fourth largest reservoir.

Before the Aswan Dam was built, farmers near the Nile River never knew if they would have enough water.

The Aswan Dam is more than two miles long! The dam also **generates** a lot of electricity.

Embankment dams

Aswan Dam is one of the largest **embankment dams** in the world. Embankment dams are made using mud and rocks with a dense, waterproof center. The dam walls have to be extra big and heavy to stand up to the force of the water.

Hoover Dam

The Hoover Dam in the United States was built during the **Great Depression**. One out of every four U.S. workers had no job, home, or money for food. This amazing project gave work to more than 20,000 people. The workers had to shift the course of the Colorado River to build the dam. It was the largest dam in the world when it was completed in 1936.

Hoover Dam

Location: Black Canyon, spanning the Colorado River between Arizona and Nevada, USA

Size: 1.24 **trillion** cubic feet (35 **billion** cubic meters)

That's Amazing!
This dam weighs more than 6.5 million tons!

The Hoover Dam was one of the world's first "super-dam" projects.

Shaped for strength

The Hoover Dam is curved. The water upstream pushes along the curve. This strengthens the dam. The walls do not need to be as thick as those for a dam that cuts straight across a river.

Lake Mead

The Hoover Dam created Lake Mead, one of the world's largest **artificial** lakes. This **reservoir** supplies the city of Las Vegas with almost 90 percent of its water.

Lake Mead can hold as much as 1.24 trillion cubic feet (35 billion cubic meters) of water.

Itaipú Dam

The Itaipú Dam in South America is really three dams joined together. It **generates** enough electricity for 10 to 12 million households! Itaipú Dam spans the Paraná River, the seventh largest river in the world. Building the dam used enough concrete to make four Hoover Dams! This was so amazing that this dam was listed as one of the "Seven Wonders of the Modern World."

Lucky Number 18
Itaipú Dam has 18 **generators**. It took 18 years and cost $18 **billion** to build.

The Itaipú Dam is nearly 5 miles (8 kilometers) long!

A large area of rain forest was lost because of this dam project.

Itaipú Dam

Location: On the Paraná River, on the border between Brazil and Paraguay

Size: 1.02 **trillion** cubic feet (29 billion cubic meters)

That's Amazing!
Until 2009, this dam was the largest power plant in the world.

Dam downside

Not everything about this dam is wonderful. More than 27,000 animals were killed in one year when they were caught in the Itaipú Dam. The dam's **reservoir** also destroyed about 270 square miles (700 square kilometers) of rain forest.

Three Gorges Dam

This huge dam in China was completed in 2008 at a cost of about $27 **billion**. The dam crosses the Yangtze River, the longest river in Asia. The Chinese government built this dam for flood control and **renewable** power. Before the dam, thousands of people died and millions became homeless whenever the Yangtze River flooded.

The Three Gorges Dam **generates** more electricity than any other dam in the world.

Three Gorges Dam
Location: China
Size: 1.45 miles (2.3 kilometers) long and 607 feet (185 meters) high
That's Amazing!
It's the world's largest dam!

Ancient Chinese legend

A gorge is a deep, narrow, rocky valley. An ancient Chinese legend tells how a goddess killed dragons to protect the peasants who lived nearby. Then she created the gorges so the Yangtze River would flow around the dragons' dead bodies.

Cliffs as high as 2,630 feet (800 meters) tower over the Yangtze River.

Fish Ladders

The Three Gorges Dam includes fish ladders. A fish ladder is a series of low steps built next to a dam. Fish can "hop" from one water-filled step to another. This helps them move up or downstream around the dam.

Grand Coulee Dam

The Grand Coulee Dam is the largest single producer of electricity in the United States. The original dam included two power plants. A third was added in 1974. The Grand Coulee is a **gravity dam**. This is like an **embankment dam**, but without the waterproof core. It needs to be super heavy to stop the flow of water.

Grand Coulee Dam

Location: Across the Columbia River, Washington State, USA

Size: 421 billion cubic feet (12 **billion** cubic meters)

That's Amazing!
It's the largest concrete structure in the world!

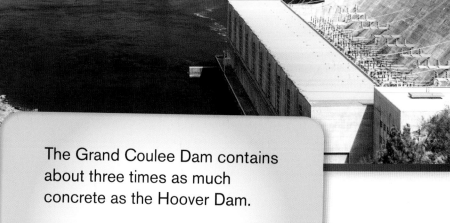

The Grand Coulee Dam contains about three times as much concrete as the Hoover Dam.

Some dams use the same building materials that go into city sidewalks.

Cement

Concrete and cement are not the same. Cement is a key ingredient in concrete. This grey powder forms the "glue" that holds the concrete together.

Concrete

Concrete is a hard building material. It is made from a mixture of cement, sand, small stones, and water. Concrete was invented thousands of years ago by the Romans.

Alqueva Dam

Before the Alqueva Dam, this part of Portugal was very dry and poor. Now, there is a reliable supply of water for homes and farms. The lake created by the dam attracts people to a new resort town, complete with golf courses!

Alqueva Dam

Location: Alentejo, Portugal

Size: 315 feet (96 meters) high, 1,503 feet (458 meters) long

That's Amazing!
This dam converted one of the poorest, driest parts of Portugal into a resort town!

50 years in the making

The idea for this dam came in 1957. Fifty years later the dam finally began working. Construction was completed in 2002. The **floodgates** were closed and water began to collect behind them. A few years later the **reservoir** reached its planned level. Today it is the largest **artificial** lake in Western Europe!

Hydroelectric Power

"Hydro" means water. **Hydroelectric** power is electricity **generated** using the force of running water. As water flows through a dam, it spins the blades of a **turbine**, which is connected to a generator that produces electricity.

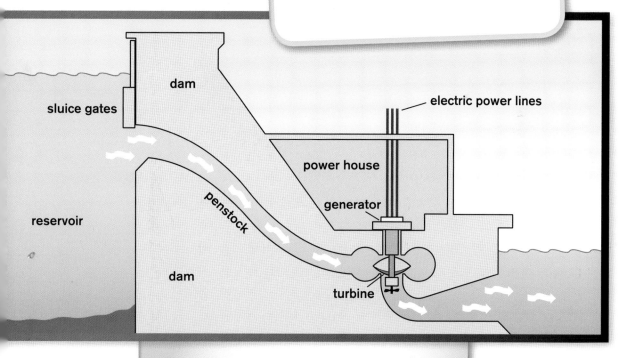

sluice gates

dam

reservoir

dam

penstock

power house

generator

turbine

electric power lines

The power plant is located near the bottom of the dam, where gravity increases the force of the moving water.

Nurek Dam

The Nurek Dam in central Asia is the tallest dam in the world. This dam across the Vakhsh River was built from 1961 to 1980 by the **Soviet Union**. Now the dam is in Tajikistan, a country founded in 1991 after the breakup of the Soviet Union. This massive dam provides people with electricity and water. A lot of the water goes to farmland so people can grow food in this dry region.

Who pays?

Huge dams take a lot of time and money to complete. Many are government projects to serve the needs of the public. Sometimes, wars or politics change a nation's borders. A place that was once part of one country becomes part of another. The government of Tajikistan could not have afforded to build this dam, which was funded by the government of the Soviet Union.

This photo shows the Nurek Dam under construction.

Nurek Dam

Location: Tajikistan, central Asia

Size: 984 feet (300 meters) high

That's Amazing!

It is currently the tallest dam in the world!

The Nurek Dam is a massive, earth-filled **embankment dam**. It supplies all the electricity for Tajikistan.

Inguri Dam

The Inguri Dam in Georgia is the highest concrete **arch dam** in the world. It was built using stacks of huge, interlocking concrete blocks. The curved shape makes a stronger dam, needing fewer building materials than a **gravity** or **embankment dam**.

Arch dams are a good choice of design for narrow, rocky valleys.

Inguri Dam

Location: Georgia, between Europe and Asia

Size: 892 feet (272 meters) high and 2,231 feet (680 meters) long

That's Amazing!
This dam spans two countries!

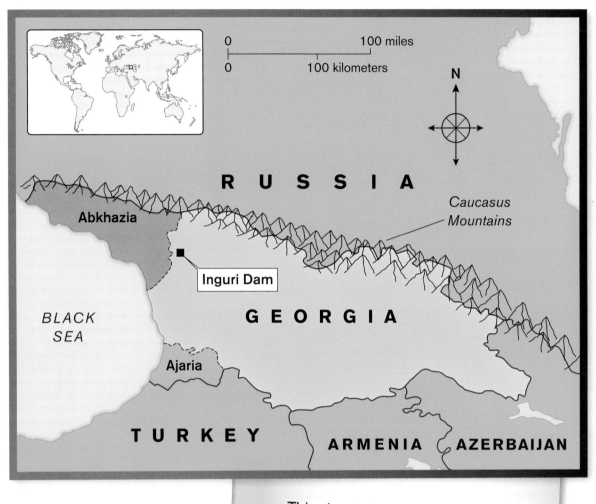

0 | 100 miles

0 | 100 kilometers

N

RUSSIA

Caucasus
Mountains

Abkhazia

Inguri Dam

BLACK
SEA

GEORGIA

Ajaria

TURKEY

ARMENIA | AZERBAIJAN

This dam is located near where the Inguri River leaves the Caucasus Mountain range.

Dam problems

This dam was built by the **Soviet Union** between 1961 and 1987. When the Soviet Union broke apart, the dam and power plant ended up on different sides of a border between two newly independent countries! Now the dam is in Georgia, but the **hydroelectric** plant is in Abkhazia. Both countries need the electricity the dam **generates**. This is the only source of electricity for Abkhazia. In 1997 Abkhazia cut off electricity to Georgia. They were protesting because Georgia had cut off their long-distance phone lines.

Nagarjuna Sagar Dam

The Nagarjuna Sagar Dam is the largest dam built from stone in the world. Construction began in 1956, but India did not have the technology to make a concrete dam then. Instead, they used stone. This took longer than building with concrete. This amazing dam is 407 feet (124 meters) high. Its unique design includes 26 separate gates along the top of the dam.

It took about 70,000 workers 13 years to build this amazing dam. Nearly 200 workers died in construction accidents.

Water for farming

Nagarjuna Sagar Dam created the third-largest **artificial** lake in the world. The dam and its canals distribute water to **irrigate** nearby land so people can grow enough food. But this came at a cost. One of India's most precious **Buddhist** sites was destroyed. It is now almost entirely under water.

Buddhist monks mourn the loss of one of their most **sacred** sites, which was destroyed by the dam.

Nagarjuna Sagar Dam

Location: Andhra Pradesh, India

Size: Reservoir holds 424,000,000 cubic feet (12 million cubic meters) of water

That's Amazing!
It is the largest dam in India, and one of the oldest.

Dam Disasters

Vajont Dam disaster, Italy, 1963

The Vajont dam tragedy in Italy was caused by a **landslide** which fell into the reservoir behind the dam. This pushed an enormous amount of water over the top of the dam. The wave was more than 820 feet (250 meters) high! More than 2,000 people died when this huge wave struck their villages. Amazingly, the dam was hardly damaged in the disaster. Only the top part was destroyed.

Vajont Dam
Location: Monte Toc, Italy
Height: 860 feet (262 meters)
Tragedy
Up to 2,500 people are believed to have died in the Vajont dam disaster of 1963. The dam is now disused.

The reservoir for the St. Francis Dam held almost 13 billion gallons of water— in those days, enough water to supply the city of Los Angeles for a year.

St. Francis Dam disaster, California, 1928

On March 12, 1928, the St. Francis Dam in California suddenly collapsed. It was the second worst disaster to hit California, second only to the 1906 earthquake and fire that destroyed the city of San Francisco. More than 450 people were killed.

The Pros and Cons of Dams

Dams are useful for flood control, creating **reservoirs**, and **generating** electricity. But they can also cause big problems for people and wildlife. Many species of fish cannot survive the water temperature changes caused by dams.

Big dams also create huge reservoirs over land that was once dry. This can lead to unexpected environmental results. For example, the reservoir for the Alqueva Dam flooded important habitats for rare plants and animals.

Rare Stone Age drawings are also now deep under water after the construction of the Alqueva Dam.

The danger of dams

More than a million Chinese people had to move because of the Three Gorges Dam. The reservoirs submerged three cities and more than 1,500 towns and villages. This massive dam project is also blamed for triggering deadly earthquakes and for killing off the Yangtze River Dolphin. This rare, 20-million-year-old species was declared **extinct** in 2007. Today some experts believe this huge dam was a big mistake.

This is a photo of the last surviving Yangtze River Dolphin. The dolphin, called Qi Qi, died in 2002.

Dams Facts and Figures

Dams are built to block the flow of river water. Big dams create huge **artificial** lakes that supply water for homes, farms, and industries. They also stop floods and **generate** electricity. Some big dams create big problems, too. Which dam do you think is the most amazing?

Aswan Dam
Location: Aswan, Egypt
Size: 6 trillion cubic feet (170 billion cubic meters)
That's Amazing!
This dam created Lake Nasser, the world's fourth largest **reservoir**.

Hoover Dam
Location: Black Canyon, spanning the Colorado River between Arizona and Nevada, USA
Size: 1.24 trillion cubic feet (35 billion cubic meters)
That's Amazing!
This dam weighs more than 6.5 million tons!

Itaipú Dam
Location: On the Paraná River, on the border between Brazil and Paraguay
Size: 1.02 trillion cubic feet (29 billion cubic meters)
That's Amazing!
Until 2009, this dam was the largest power plant in the world.

Three Gorges Dam
Location: China
Size: 1.45 miles (2.3 kilometers) long and 607 feet (185 meters) high
That's Amazing!
It's the world's largest dam!

Grand Coulee Dam

Location: Across the Columbia River, Washington State, USA

Size: 421 billion cubic feet (12 **billion** cubic meters)

That's Amazing!
It's the largest concrete structure in the world!

Alqueva Dam

Location: Alentejo, Portugal

Size: 315 feet (96 meters) high, 1,503 feet (458 meters) long

That's Amazing!
This dam converted one of the poorest, driest parts of Portugal into a resort town!

Nurek Dam

Location: Tajikistan, central Asia

Size: 984 feet (300 meters) high

That's Amazing!
It is currently the tallest dam in the world!

Inguri Dam

Location: Georgia, between Europe and Asia

Size: 892 feet (272 meters) high and 2,231 feet (680 meters) long

That's Amazing!
This dam spans two countries!

Nagarjuna Sagar Dam

Location: Andhra Pradesh, India

Size: Reservoir holds 424,000,000 cubic feet (12 million cubic meters) of water

That's Amazing!
It is the largest dam in India, and one of the oldest.

Vajont Dam

Location: Monte Toc, Italy

Height: 860 feet (262 meters)

Tragedy
Up to 2,500 people are believed to have died in the Vajont dam disaster of 1963. The dam is not used now.

Glossary

arch dam dam with a curved shape, designed so that water pressure strengthens the structure

artificial made by humans

billion thousand million

Buddhist person who follows the religion of Buddhism

embankment dam big, heavy dam made of mud and rocks with a dense, waterproof center

extinct died out

floodgates part of a dam that opens and closes, like a gate to control the flow of water

generate produce electricity

gravity dam straight dam built thick, heavy, and strong enough to block water with its weight

Great Depression time in history (1929–1939) when there was mass unemployment and poverty

hydroelectric to do with making electricity using the pressure of falling water

irrigate water farms so crops grow

landslide soil and rocks sliding down a hillside

renewable kind of power, or energy, that does not run out because it is based on something that continues to renew, or refresh, itself. Water, wind, and solar power are renewable.

reservoir lake formed when a dam is built across a river

sacred to do with religion

Soviet Union Communist state made up of Russia and its former empire. The Soviet Union broke up in 1991.

trillion million million

turbine motor with blades that are turned by the motion of air or water

Find Out More

Books

Aldridge, Rebecca. *The Hoover Dam*. New York, NY: Chelsea House, 2009.

Kite, Patricia L. *Building the Three Gorges Dam*. Chicago, IL: Raintree, 2011.

Mullins, Matt. *How Did They Build That?* Ann Arbor, Mich.: Cherry Lake, 2010.

Phillips, Cynthia and Shana Priwer. *Dams and Waterways*. Armonk, NY: M.E. Sharpe, 2009.

Websites

http://tiki.oneworld.net/energy/energy8.html
Find out more about renewable energy.

http://www.pbs.org/wgbh/buildingbig/dam/
This section of the PBS website is all about dams.

http://www.sciencekids.co.nz/sciencefacts/engineering/dams.html
More about dams, and why they are built.

http://www.tvakids.com/river/aboutdams.htm
The kids' page of the Tennessee Valley Authority website has a lot of information about dams.

Index